Man's Approach
to God

Man's Approach to God

by Jacques Maritain

Wimmer Lecture V

THE ARCHABBEY PRESS

Latrobe, Pennsylvania

Distributed by

University Publishers, Inc.
59 East 54th Street
New York 22, N.Y.

Wimmer Lecture V

Saint Vincent College
Latrobe, Pennsylvania

The Wimmer Lecture

During the centenary year of Saint Vincent
Archabbey and College the Board of Trustees
of the College established an annual lecture
in honor of the Right Reverend Archabbot
Boniface Wimmer, O.S.B. It was on Octo-
ber 18, 1846, that Boniface Wimmer, with
his small band of Pioneers, arrived at St.
Vincent and began the first permanent Benedictine foundation in North America. From
this archabbey numerous other Benedictine
abbeys have sprung, directly or indirectly.
They carry on the monastic life and conduct
schools and colleges in many parts of the
United States and Canada.

By a memorial at once fitting and significant
the Wimmer Lecture seeks to keep alive and
in grateful remembrance the name of this
good and great man. Each year on some
convenient day, preferably near December
8th, the anniversary of his death, it brings

before the members of the institution he founded a distinguished scholar, whose lecture is subsequently printed in the form of a small book. The lecturer is free to choose his own subject.

Following is the list of Wimmer Lecturers with their topics:

Man's Approach
to God

I

MAY I SUGGEST, AS A PRELIMINARY remark, that in order to get a sufficiently comprehensive notion of the problems which have to do with our knowledge of the existence of God, we must take into account both that approach to God which depends on the natural forces of the human mind and that approach to God which depends on the supernatural gift of faith. Only thus can we have a complete picture of the subject.

Consequently, I shall have to complement my philosophical discussion, in this lecture, with some considerations borrowed from theology.

1. Physics is today reigning unchallenged over our minds and culture. Its progress and achievements are actually wonderful and deserve deep admiration. What is badly needed is not to disparage physics and accuse it of atomizing us, but to be aware of its very nature, its true field of knowledge and its limitations. What is badly needed is to supplement physics with another type of knowledge, concerned with grasping being for its own sake. What is badly needed is a renewal of metaphysics.

No doubt there is no continuity between the world of physics and the world of metaphysics. The modern image of the atom—each day more complicated, more mysterious and more fecund in practical applications—is a mathematical image or ideal entity founded on reality, which gives us an invaluable symbolical or phenomenological knowledge of *how matter behaves,* but cannot instruct us philosophically or ontologically about *what matter is.* Yet the fact remains that the conceptions of modern science and the extraordinary progress of micro-physics provide the human intellect with a scientific imagery, an imaginable or supra-imaginable picture of nature which is incomparably more favorable to the edification of a philosophy of nature and more open to the deepening labor of metaphysical reason than the old Newtonian physics. The opportunity is now given for that reconciliation between science and wisdom for which the human mind thirsts.

The "*existential*" philosophies which are today in fashion are but a sign of a certain deep want to find again the sense of Being. This want remains, however, unfulfilled, for these philosophies are still enslaved by irrationalism and seek for the revelation of existence, for ontological ecstasy, in the breaking of reason, in the experience of despair and nothingness, of anguish or absurdity. True existentialism is the work of reason.[1]

It is so because the primary reality grasped by the intellect is the act of existing as exercised by some visible or tangible thing; and because it is the intuition of being—disengaged for its own sake, and perceived at the summit of an abstractive intellection—it is the intuition of being—even when it is distorted by the error of a system, as in Plato or Spinoza—which causes a human intellect to enter the realm of metaphysics and be capable of metaphysical intelligence.

2. From Plato and Aristotle to St. Anselm and St. Thomas Aquinas, Descartes and Leibniz, philosophers offered proofs or demonstrations of God's existence, or, as Thomas Aquinas more modestly and accurately puts it, *ways* of making God's existence intellectually sure—all of them are highly conceptualized and rationalized, specifically *philosophical* ways of approach. Kant criticized the proof afforded by Descartes, the so-called ontological argument, and wrongly endeavored to reduce all other ways of demonstration to this particular one, so as to envelop them in the same condemnation.[2] This was a great mistake, for the five ways pointed out by Thomas Aquinas are totally independent of the ontological argument; they hold true before any criticism, and are unshakeably valid in themselves.

Yet I do not intend to consider now these

highly conceptualized and rationalized, specifically *philosophical* ways of approach. When
St. Paul asserted: "What is known about God
is clear to them [namely, to the Gentiles], for
God Himself has made it clear, for since the
creation of the world His invisible attributes
—His everlasting power and divinity—are to
be discerned and contemplated through His
works,"[3] he was not only concerned with the
scientifically elaborated or specifically philosophical ways of establishing God's existence,
but also, and first of all, with the natural
knowledge of God's existence to which the
vision of created things leads the reason of
any man whatsoever, be he a philosopher or
not. It is this natural knowledge of God's
existence that I shall consider—a knowledge
which is natural not only in the sense of
rational or non-supernatural, but also in the

sense of *naturally* or *pre*-philosophically ac-
quired, or prior to any philosophical, scientifically rationalized elaboration.

In other words I submit that, before the
human mind enters the sphere of perfectly
formed and articulate knowledge, particu-
larly the sphere of metaphysical knowledge,
it is capable of a pre-philosophical knowledge
which is *virtually metaphysical*. It is this pre-
philosophical knowledge that I shall now try
to outline, at least in a tentative way.[4]

3. What must be first of all stressed in this
connection is, I think, the fact that, once a
man is awakened to the reality of existence,
once he has really perceived this tremendous
fact, sometimes exhilarating, sometimes dis-
gusting and maddening, namely: I *exist,* he is
henceforth taken hold of by the intuition of
Being and the implications it involves.

Precisely speaking, this prime intuition is both the intuition of *my* existence and of the existence of things; but first and foremost of the existence of things. When it takes place, I suddenly realize that a given entity, man, mountain, or tree, exists and exercises that sovereign activity *to be* in its own way, totally self-assertive and totally implacable, compeletely independent from *me*. And at the same time I realize that I also exist but as thrown back into my loneliness and frailty by such affirmation of existence in which I have positively no part, to which I am exactly as naught. So the prime intuition of Being is the intuition of the solidity and inexorability of existence; and, secondly, of the death and nothingness to which *my* existence is liable. And thirdly, in the same flash of intuition, which is but my *becoming aware* of the intelligible value of Being, I realize that the solid and inexorable existence perceived in anything whatsoever implies—I don't know yet in what way, perhaps in things themselves, perhaps separately from them—some absolute, irrefragable existence, completely free from nothingness and death. These three intellective leaps—to actual existence as asserting itself independently from me; from this sheer objective existence to my own threatened existence; and from my existence spoiled with nothingness to absolute existence—are achieved within that same and unique intuition which philosophers would explain as the intuitive perception of the essentially analogical content of the first concept, the concept of Being.

Then—this is the second step—a quick, spontaneous reasoning, as natural as this intuition (and, as a matter of fact, more or less involved in it) immediately springs forth, as the necessary fruit of such primordial apperception and as enforced by and under its light. I see that my Being, *first,* is liable to death; and, second, that it depends on the totality of nature, on the universal whole whose part I am; and that Being-with-nothingness, as my own being is, implies, in order to be, Being-without-nothingness. It implies that absolute existence which I confusedly perceived as involved in my primordial intuition of existence. Now the universal whole, whose part I am, is Being-with-nothingness from the very fact that I am part of it; consequently it does not exist by itself. And thus, finally, since the universal whole does not exist by itself, there is another, separate, whole, another Being, transcendent and self-sufficient and unknown in itself and activating all beings, which is Being-without-nothingness, that is, Being by itself.

Thus the inner dynamism of the intuition of existence, or of the intelligible value of Being, causes me to see that absolute existence or Being-without-nothingness transcends the totality of nature, and compels me to face the existence of God.

This is not a new approach to God. It is the eternal approach of man's reason to God. What is new is the manner in which the modern mind has become aware of the simplicity and liberating power, the natural and somehow intuitive characteristics of this eternal approach. The science of the ancients was steeped in philosophy. Their scientific imagery was a pseudo-ontological imagery. Consequently there was a kind of continuum between their knowledge of the physical world and their knowledge of God. The latter appeared as the summit of the former, a summit which was to be climbed through the manifold paths of the causal connections at play in the sublunar world and the celestial spheres. The sense of Being that ruled their universal thought was for them a too usual atmosphere to be felt as a surprising gift. At the same time the natural intuition of existence was so strong in them that their proofs of God could take the form of the most conceptualized and rationalized scientific demonstrations, and be offered as an unrolling of logical necessities, without losing the inner energy of that intuition. Such logical machinery was quickened instinctively by the basic intuition of Being.

We are in a quite different position now. In order to solve the enigma of physical reality and to conquer the world of phenomena, our science has become a kind of Maya—a Maya which succeeds and makes us masters of nature. But the sense of Being is absent from it. Thus when we happen to experience the impact of Being upon the mind it appears to us as a kind of intellectual revelation, and we realize clearly both its liberating and its awakening power and the fact that it involves a knowledge which is separated from that sphere of knowledge peculiar to our science. At the same time we realize that the knowledge of God, before being developed into logical and perfectly conceptualized demonstrations, is first and foremost a natural fruit of the intuition of existence, and forces itself upon our mind in the imperative virtue of this intuition.

In other words, we have become aware of

the fact that human reason's approach to God, in its primordial vitality, is neither a mere intuition, which would be suprahuman, nor is it that artlike philosophical reasoning by which it is expressed in its achieved form, each step of which is pregnant with involved issues and problems. Human reason's approach to God in its primordial vitality is a *natural* reasoning, that is, intuitive-like or irresistibly vitalized by, and maintained within, the intellectual flash of the intuition of existence. Then the intuition of existence, grasping in some existing reality Being-with-nothingness, makes the mind grasp by the same stroke the necessity of Being-without-nothingness. And nowhere is there any problem involved, because the illumining power of this intuition takes hold of the mind and obliges it to see. Thus it naturally proceeds, in a primary intuitive flash, from imperative certainty to imperative certainty. I believe that from Descartes to Kierkegaard, the effort of modern thought—to the extent that it has not completely repudiated metaphysics, and if it is cleansed of the irrationalism which has gradually corrupted it—tends to such an awareness of the specific *naturality* of man's knowledge of God, definitely deeper than any logical process scientifically developed. It tends to the awareness of man's spontaneous knowledge of God, and of the primordial and simple intuitivity in which it originates.

4. I have just tried to describe the way in which this *natural* pre-philosophical knowledge spontaneously proceeds. It implies a reasoning, but an intuitive-like reasoning, steeped in the primordial intuition of existence. I would say that this natural knowledge

is a kind of *innocent* knowledge—I mean pure of any dialectics. Such knowledge involves certitude, cogent certitude, but in an imperfect logical state; it has not crossed the threshold of *scientific* demonstration, the certitude of which is critical and implies the logical overcoming of the difficulties involved; and by the same token such natural knowledge is still blissfully ignorant of these difficulties, of all that burden of objections which St. Thomas puts at the beginning of his demonstrations. Because scientific certitude and objections to be met—and the answers to the objections—come into being together.

We see, then, that the philosophical proofs of the existence of God, say, the five ways of Thomas Aquinas, are a development and explication of this natural knowledge on the level of scientific discussion and scientific certitude. And they normally presuppose this natural knowledge, not as regards the logical structure of the demonstration, but as regards the existential condition of the thinking subject. Thus, if all the preceding observations are true, we should always—before offering the philosophical proofs, say, the classical five ways[5]—make sure that those we are addressing are awakened to the primordial intuition of existence and aware of the natural knowledge of God involved in it.

Let us mention now that there are two other pre-philosophical approaches to God—namely, through art and poetry, and through moral experience.

As concerns art and poetry, suffice it to quote the famous page where Baudelaire has translated into his own language a passage from a lecture by Edgar Allan Poe, on *The Poetic*

Principle. It is the immortal instinct for beauty, he said, ''which makes us consider the world and its pageants as a glimpse of, a correspondence with, Heaven. . . . It is at once by poetry and *through* poetry, by music and *through* music, that the soul divines what splendors shine behind the tomb, and when an exquisite poem brings tears to the eyes, such tears are not the sign of an excess of joy, they are rather a witness of an irritated melancholy, an exigency of nerves, a nature exiled in the imperfect which would possess immediately, on this very earth, a paradise revealed.''[6] *Our art*, Dante said, *is the grandchild of God*. The poet completes the work of creation; he co-operates in divine balancings, he moves mysteries about; he is in natural sympathy with the secret powers that play about in the universe. A slide down the inclined plane of heaven, a push from grace: the sleeper will change sides, and will wake up with God.

In the last analysis all genuine poetry is religious. Even if a poet has no conceptual knowledge of God, even if he is or believes he is an atheist, it is toward the primary source of Beauty that in actual fact his spiritual effort is oriented. And thus, if no intellectual or moral hindrance thwarts this spiritual dynamism, he will naturally be led by poetry to some conscious notion and awareness of the existence of that God at Whom he is unconsciously looking, in and through his art and his work.

As concerns moral experience, we may observe that when a man experiences, in a primary act of freedom, the impact of the moral good, and is thus awakened to moral existence, and directs his life toward the good for the sake of the good, then he directs his life, without knowing it, toward the absolute Good, and in this way knows God vitally, by virtue of the inner dynamism of his choice of the good, even if he does not know God in any conscious fashion or by means of any conceptual knowledge.[7] Let us suppose that no intellectual prejudice, deformation, or illusion thwarts this spiritual dynamism, and that no erroneous representation causes what is implied in the dynamism in question to be seemingly denied by conceptual thought: then the man who has really chosen the good for the sake of the good will be led by moral experience to some conscious notion and awareness of that God at Whom he is unconsciously looking in and through his primary act of freedom.

Moral experience in which man deliberating

about himself chooses the moral good, *bonum honestum,* the end of his life—artistic creation which engenders in beauty—intuitive grasping of the intelligible value of the act of existing— these three approaches are existential approaches; they plunge into real existence. But the privilege of the intuition of being is that it winds up directly in a conscious and conceptually expressed, irrefragable awareness of the existence of God.

It also carries along with itself another intuition, the intuition of the Self, of subjectivity as subjectivity, which is at the same time a discovery of the basic generosity of existence. For "it is better to give than to receive"; and that kind of spiritual existence which consists in love and the gift of oneself is the supreme revelation of existence for the Self.

Man's Approach to God

But is it not impossible that the supreme
cause of existence should not enjoy the supreme kind of existence? So man awakened
to the sense of being does not only know that
God exists and is self-subsisting Existence, he
also knows that because of this very fact God
is absolute ontological generosity and self-
subsisting love; and that such transcendent
love causes, permeates, and activates every
creature.

Though human reason is helped in fact by
revelation to know more perfectly these
natural truths, reason is enough, the natural
forces of the human mind are enough, for
man to know that God is self-subsisting Love,
as He is self-subsisting Intellection and self-
subsisting Existence. And we also know,
through the Gospel revelation, through faith,
that, as far as the creature is concerned, God

should not only be loved but that He loves, I mean with the distinctive *madness* of love, and that there can be relations of friendship, mutual self-giving, community of life, and the sharing of a common bliss between God and His intelligent creatures: a fact which implies the supernatural order of grace and charity.

II

5. I am coming to the second part of this lecture—so we are confronted with one knowledge of God which depends solely on reason and the natural forces of the human intellect, and another knowledge of God which is knowledge by faith and deals with the supernatural order.

Knowledge by faith is obscure knowledge,

knowledge in an imperfect state, because faith believes and does not see. Faith, which is a gift of God, implies the action of divine grace which innerly inspires and illumines the intellect and moves the will; it is the adherence of the intellect to truths and realities which are above the range of reason, and are believed as spoken and witnessed by the word of God, the Prime Truth itself. So the mode of knowledge by faith is imperfect, but its *object* is more valuable than anything reason can know—its object is the hidden treasure involved in the very essence of God and His own knowledge of Himself.[8]

On the contrary, knowledge of God as afforded by reason is clear and obvious knowledge, springing forth from the first intuition of being with cogent force. Be it either merely spontaneous or philosophically elaborated, its mode is luminous, not obscure. But the object it attains is God known only as through His effects, or as the primary Cause of things can be made manifest by the very same ideas through which things are first known—God known *not* in Himself, but in the mirror of things, God in the analogical community of His being with the being of creatures.[9]

No doubt faith also is knowledge through analogy as regards the *means* or the human *concepts* it uses. But analogy, there, does not determine the very content offered to knowledge, or the formal objectivity with which God faces the intellect, and which is the divine essence itself, the inner mystery of God as known to Himself. In faith, analogy, or rather super-analogy, deals only with the signs and means that bring such an object within our understanding.[10] To express the mystery of the Trinity, for example, it is necessary to make use of the concepts of Father, and Son, and Spirit, of generation and procession, concepts which were first supplied to us by creatures, and which God Himself uses in making Himself known to us through His Son who tells of Him, and through His Church which guards and explains the word of the Son: analogical concepts by means of which *lumen fidei,* the light of faith, reaches the inwardness of God. These concepts are the *outward silver,* as St. John of the Cross put it, by means of which we grasp the *pure gold* of divine reality.[11] Let us say, then, that faith dwells in the divine fountainhead itself, in the heart of the Increate, but that God has laid His hand over her eyes.

In contrast, merely rational and natural

knowledge of God dwells in the created world, and from there gazes—without seeing it in itself—at the inaccessible source toward which all perfections of created things converge, and whose pure light natural reason can only grasp as broken in the multiplicity of those perfections. In the rational and natural knowledge of God the analogical process is the very measure and rule of knowledge. God is not attained in the name of His Self-hood and incommunicable nature, or of the indivisibility of His pure and simple essence, but only to the extent that He is manifested in the reflected hues and analogical participations which things proportioned to our reason offer us. His essence is not attained as such, but only to the extent that creatures speak of it from themselves to our intellect. Thus not only is the mode of this kind of knowledge human, but its very object is proposed to the mind and constituted as the aim of knowledge only insofar as it condescends, so to speak, to human reason through the mirror of sense-perceivable things and through the analogy of being.

6. I should like to dwell a moment on this natural knowledge of God, either spontaneous or philosophical, and to give a few indications of its analogical character.

In all things that we see and touch there are certain objects of thought, brought out by our intellectual power of conceptual apprehension, which are called *transcendental* objects of thought, because they transcend and overflow any genus and category, they know no bounds. Such is, first of all, being—our first object of thought. Such objects of thought as *being, unity, truth, beauty* imbue each and every thing, including the very differences through which things are distinct from each other.[12] As a result, these transcendentals, which are restricted to no thing whatever, imply in their very notion neither limitation nor imperfection; and they are ascribed to things essentially varied—to a man, to a color, to a physical energy, to a spiritual power—in an analogous, not a univocal manner. In each one of those things they do not signify one single generic or specific nature, but something intrinsically varied, namely, a similarity in relations between similar terms; for instance: the essence of man is to his own existence as the essence of a spark of light or a melody is to its own existence.

Thus it is that such notions can be ascribed to God: being, truth, or beauty are limited and imperfect *in things,* but they do not imply any limitation or imperfection *in their very notion.* They therefore can and must be ascribed to the one who is infinite and infinitely perfect— the prime cause of every being and every beauty is really being—the very act of existing subsisting through itself—and is really true, and truth itself, beautiful, and beauty itself.

Being, truth, and beauty do not imply any community of essence in the various things that exist, and are true, and are beautiful. They can therefore be ascribed to God without jeopardizing in any way the absolute and infinite difference in essence between God and the things in which we first deciphered these notions. They imply between God and things no univocal identity whatsoever, only *analogous* community.

Let us now point out that our knowledge of God—and this is true for the super-analogy of faith-knowledge as well as for the analogy of reason-knowledge—let us now point out that our knowledge of God does not only proceed through analogy. It must be added that this analogy is uncontaining, *uncircumscriptive*.[13] The concepts and names which designate perfections pertaining to the transcendental order do not vanish, do not fly into pieces, they keep their proper significance when applied to God. But although coming into effect far better in God than in things, they neither enclose nor embrace the divine reality, they leave it uncontained and uncircumscribed. *What is signified* by our analogous concepts pertains to God, and in a better way than to things. But *the manner in which we conceive* them, with the limitations it inevitably involves (since we have received those concepts from creatures), the *modus significandi* does in no way pertain to God. God is truly *ipsum esse per se subsistens,* Being itself subsisting through itself, but He does not suffer any of the circumscribing marks implied in our manner of conceiving being, insofar as we conceive being as distinct from goodness, truth, or beauty. God exists, but He does not exist as do any of the existing things. God is good and just and merciful, God knows, God loves, but He is not good, just, or merciful, he does not know or love as any of the beings are or do which have taught us what is goodness, justice or mercy, knowledge or love. In the very degree to which they make the divine essence known to us, our concepts, while keeping their proper meaning, are absorbed into its abyss. In God what is signified by them breaks loose—we don't know how—from *our manner of conceiving.* The

divine essence is known in some fashion—
and truly known—but it does not surrender
itself; its own mystery remains intact, un-
pierced. To the very extent to which we
know it, it escapes our grasp, infinitely transcends our knowledge. As St. Thomas put it
after Augustine and Boethius, "Whatever
form our intellect may conceive, God escapes
it through His own sublimity."[14]

III

7. It is time to pass to the third and final
part of this lecture. Through the natural
forces or our intellect we know that God
exists, as primary Cause of things; we know
God in and by His effects, but we do not
know Him in and by His essence.

But it is but normal that knowing a reality—

and the most important one—from the out-
side and by means of signs, we have a desire
to know it *in itself*, or to grasp it without
intermediary. So we have a natural desire to
see in His essence that very God whom we
know through His creatures.[15]

Yet such a longing to know the first Cause
in its essence is a longing which does not
know what it is asking—like the sons of
Zebedee when they asked to sit on the right
and the left hand of the Son of Man—because
to know the first Cause in its essence—or
without the medium of any other thing—
means ceasing to know it through its effects,
or insofar as it is Cause and first Cause, that
is, ceasing to use the very way through which
our intellect has come to know it and is facing
it. To know the first Cause in its essence is
in reality something which transcends all the

forces of any created or creatable nature, it is identical with possessing the deity intuitively, in a vision in which the divine essence itself plays within our mind the part of our concepts as means of grasping intelligible objects; to know God in His essence is to know God divinely, as he is known to Himself; it is to know Him as He knows us, in His own uncreated light. To see God is supernatural, is even at the peak of the supernatural order. To see God is possible only for a divinized mind, for a mind whose subjective intellectual power is proportioned to God by that supreme participation in God's life which is called *lumen gloriae*,[16] the light of glory—for a mind whose objective intentional determination depends on nothing created, on no idea, but on the divine essence itself. Such perfect intuition is so supernatural that through it man becomes God intentionally, in the pure spirituality of this eternal intellectual act, and that through it man possesses beatitude, and enters God's very joy, an absolute happiness which, with respect to our merely natural possibilities, we could not dare to dream of.

So, when Thomas Aquinas says that if it were impossible for man to see God a natural desire would be bound to remain vain, he does not mean that the vision of God is in the natural range of our intellect, he means that the possibility for an act which is essentially supernatural must exist in man—in other words he intends to show that there exists in our intellect a *potentia obedientialis,* a root potentiality—facing the omnipotence of God —to be divinely raised beyond all that its nature is capable of.

The longing to see God, when it is a desire

which knows what it is asking, when it tends to God *as God, and as opening up His essence to the eyes of man,* is a supernatural longing rooted in supernatural faith, and distinct from the natural desire, tending to God as *first Cause,* of which I spoke a moment ago. It is grafted on this natural desire, and it also perfects and superelevates our natural desire for happiness, now become desire for bliss. But in itself it is supernatural.

8. Thus it is that faith is a movement toward vision. Thus it is that in the dynamism of our grace-given energies, faith, which by itself can only believe, but neither penetrate nor experience, demands to be vitally complemented by other supernatural virtues—the gifts of the Holy Spirit—which, thanks to the connaturality of love, make faith penetrate and experience the divine reality, and so to

speak give eyes to faith—*fides oculata*.[17] For "where love is, there also are eyes." So divine contemplation is here below a token and shadow, an experienced promise of vision.

We are co-natured with God by charity. The things of God having been thus intimately joined with us, made ours, bred into our bones by the love of charity, the property of the gift of wisdom is to *make use of this love* to make it grow into an *objective means* of knowing,[18] in such a way that we not only experience our love, but it is God Himself whom we experience through our love. As John of St. Thomas put it,

> By virtue of this union by which love adheres immediately to God, the intellect is raised by a certain affective experience to the point of judging of divine things in a higher manner than is possible for the obscurity of faith, because the intellect penetrates and knows that there is *still more* hidden sub-

stance in the things of faith than faith itself can
manifest, and because it finds there *more* to love
and to taste in love; and from this *more* which is
hidden there, as the intellect knows through love,
the intellect judges of divine things in a higher
fashion, by a special instinct of the Holy Spirit.'[19]

We see, then, that mystical wisdom pene-
trates the things of God by an experience of
love which bears on that very substance which
is hidden in faith. It is in the very degree to
which divine reality is hidden to us—abso-
lutely transcendent with respect to any concept or idea—that this secret wisdom experiences it. Truly Thou art a hidden God, a
Saviour God: all the more Saviour and Vivifier
as He is hidden. The man of contemplation
cherishes these dark shadows of faith because
he knows that they are fecund, because he
knows, he feels, that only in them can he
intimately taste and judge by experience the

depths of his God. Here we are at the root of the doctrine of St. John of the Cross:

> Seek Him in faith and love, like a blind man these two guides will lead you, by roads you do not know, up to the secret of God.[20] . . . He is hidden in you, why do you not hide yourself like Him in order to know Him and to feel Him? If a man wants to find something hidden, he must hide himself in entering its hiding place, and when he has found it he is hidden like it.[21] . . . Always you must hold Him to be hidden, and serve Him by hiding yourself.[22]

In such an experience the concepts are not suppressed; but all distinct concepts keep silent, they sleep, as the Apostles slept on the Mount of Olives. And the confused concepts which intervene, and which may remain wholly unperceived, play a merely accidental part. It is the connaturality of charity which plays the essential part, is the formal and decisive means of knowledge. The light of

God-given contemplation is the ardor of love gleaming in the dark. That is why this supreme wisdom, this supernatural knowledge of love, is described as a giving up of knowledge and an unknowing, *a ray of darkness for the intellect.*[23] As St. Thomas puts it, quoting the Pseudo-Dionysius, "At the summit of our knowledge we know God *as unknown.*"[24] He is known as unknown, *tanquam ignotus cognoscitur.* He is known as infinitely transcending any human or angelic knowledge; that is to say, He is known precisely *as God,* in the incomprehensible depths themselves of His deity. He is actually known—while remaining unknown and inscrutable. All particular representations have vanished away, the soul has given up everything, and given up itself. The God of faith is experienced by his reverberation, His implanting in love.

9. I have tried to explain these things at greater length in a book—*The Degrees of Knowledge*—which I beg you not to read, for the English translation is full of deadly distortions of the original meaning.[25] Now I should like to add that for the Christian philosophy of life contemplation—I mean that supernatural contemplation of which I just spoke, and which would be better called entrance into the very states of God, of God Incarnate—is not the business only of specialists or the chosen few. It is a promise to all men. Compared with the pre-Christian world, this was an astounding revolution in the *spiritual order*.

All without exception are called to the perfection of love; and that perfection cannot be attained without the radical purifications and substantial remoldings which only contemplative experience, in which man is dispossessed of himself and led by superior inspiration, can provide. As a result, this experience of divine things requests no doubt that certain men be especially dedicated to it in a uniquely contemplative state of life, but it likewise seeks to spread over the world and attract to itself all men, provided they have the will to enter the ways of the spirit, and whatever their state of life may be.[26] For in whatever work they are engaged, their action can, at least as regards the *manner* in which it is done, spring from the super-abundance of contemplation, if their soul habitually makes room for the divine inspiration. Such is the teaching of the theologians from whom my philosophy likes to get its schooling.

They must observe furthermore that among the inspiring gifts which we have learned to enumerate from Isaiah, some, like those of Counsel, Force, Fear, mainly concern action, while others, like those of Intelligence and Wisdom, are mainly related to contemplation.

It follows that souls which have entered the ways of spiritual life will behave in very different manners, each according to its calling. Some will be favored in a pre-eminent manner with the highest gifts, those of Wisdom and Intelligence: they will have the grace of contemplation in its typical forms. In the case of other souls it will be primarily the other gifts of inspired freedom: it is pre-eminently in relation to their activities and works that they will experience the effects of those gifts.

They will not be, for all that, deprived of contemplation. Their contemplation will be *masked*, or unapparent, but they will have contemplative graces. Perhaps they will be

capable only of falling asleep when they cease
moving, and mental prayer will bring them
only headaches. Mysterious contemplation
will not be in their way of praying but in the
grace of their behavior—in their sweet-
minded hands, perhaps, or perhaps in their
way of walking, or in their way of looking at
a poor man or at suffering.[27]

To conclude I should like to indicate, at
this point, that what we are taught by the
experience and example of the men and
women who are now bringing the testimony
of the Gospel into dockyards and factories, is
the fact that love for our neighbor is, like love
for God, a way and means to become con-
natured with God and to know Him through
connaturality and that all the purifications,
trials, and experiences conducing to divine
union, which the great Doctors in spirituality

have described in the progress of the supernatural love for God, are paralleled in the
progress of the supernatural love for our
fellowmen.[28] For the two great command-
ments, in which all the Law and the Prophets
consist, are but one commandment; love for
God and love for our brothers are one single
love of charity.

Thus a new mode or style of contemplation
and contemplative life is developing, in which
man—far from separating himself from the
world in solitude, and seeking to forget it
(except in praying for his brothers)—con-
tinues to share in the daily labor, trials, and
sufferings of other men, and draws all this to
God while retiring within himself to con-
verse with Him and know Him through union.
Then contemplative life permeates the chores
of common existence and emerges from them

as the repose which comes after work, and as a secret fruit of the love which quickens it. The anxieties and moans of fraternal charity vibrate as overtones in the very contemplation of divine things; the Gospel is met, and the humanity of Christ is looked at, in every decision to be made with respect to the needs and wounds of any man on the road; and it is through their impact on the compassion for, and understanding of, the creatures enveloped in divine love, that the gifts of Intelligence and Wisdom lead the soul to the contemplation of God and impart to it some experience of the ineffable Absolute.

Notes

1. Cf. Étienne Gilson, *L'Être et l'Essence,* Paris, Vrin, 1948; and my book *Existence and the Existent,* New York, Pantheon Books, 1948.

2. Cf. my book *The Dream of Descartes,* New York, Philosophical Library, 1944, ch. IV.

3. Rom. 1: 19–20.

4. Cf. my essay "A New Approach to God" in *Our Emergent Civilization,* ed. Ruth Nanda Anshen, New York, Harper, 1947; and *Approches de Dieu,* Paris, Alsatia, 1953.

5. Cf. *Summa theologica,* I, q. 2, a. 3; R. Garrigou-Lagrange, *Dieu, son existence et sa nature,* 6e édition, Paris, Beauchesne, 1933; R. Garrigou-Lagrange, *Le Sens Commun, la Philosophie de l'être et les formules dogmatiques,* 4e édition, Paris, Desclée De Brouwer, 1936; and my book *Approches de Dieu.*

6. Charles Baudelaire, "Théophile Gautier," in *L'Art Romantique.*

7. Cf. my book, *The Range of Reason,* New York, Scribner's, 1952, ch. VI; St. Thomas Aquinas, *Summa theologica,* I–II, q. 89, a. 6, and Cajetan's Commentary on this article.

8. Cf. St. Thomas Aquinas, *De Veritate,* q. 14; *Summa theologica,* II–II, q. 1 and 2 (especially q. 1, a. 2, corp. and ad 2).

9. Cf. St. Thomas Aquinas, *Summa theologica,* I, q. 13, a. 3 and 5; *Summa contra Gent.,* I, 30; *De Potentia,* q. 7, a. 5.

10. Cf. my book *Les Degrés du Savoir,* Paris, Desclée De Brouwer, 1932, pp. 478–483, 493–499.

11. St. John of the Cross, *Canticle,* str. 12.

12. Cf. St. Thomas Aquinas, *De Veritate,* q. 1, a. 1.

13. Cf. St. Thomas Aquinas, *Summa theologica,* I, q. 13, a. 5.

14. *Quamcumque formam intellectus concipiat, Deus subterfugit illam per suam eminentiam.* St. Thomas Aquinas, *In I. Sent.*, dist. 22, q. 1, a. 1. Cf. *De Potentia*, q. 7, a. 5, ad 13.

15. *Summa theologica*, I, q. 12, a. 1 and 4. Cf. my books *Les Degrés du Savoir*, p. 562, note 1, and *Approches de Dieu*, ch. V.

16. *Summa theologica*, I, q. 12, a. 5.

17. Cf. R. Garrigou-Lagrange, *Perfection Chrétienne et Contemplation*, Paris, Desclée et Cie, t. II, pp. 110–111, apropos of *Sum. theol.*, III, q. 55, a. 2, ad 1.

18. *Et sic affectus transit in conditionem objecti.* John of St. Thomas, *Cursus theologicus*, I–II, q. 68–70, disp. 18, a, 4, n. 11.

19. John of St. Thomas, *Cursus theologicus*, ibid., n. 14 (French translation by Raïssa Maritain, *Les Dons du Saint-Esprit*, Paris, Téqui, 1950, p. 100; English translation by Rev. Dominic Hughes, *The Gifts of the Holy Ghost*, New York, Sheed and Ward, 1951, p. 129).

20. St. John of the Cross, *Canticle,* str. 1, second redaction, Silv., III, p. 201–202.

21. *Ibid.,* p. 200.

22. *Ibid.,* p. 203.

23. Cf. St. John of the Cross (quoting the Pseudo-Dionysius), *Living Flame,* str. 3, verse 3, second redaction, Silv., IV, p. 181–183 (72–73); *Canticle,* str. 13 (14), Silv., III., p. 73.

24. Dionysius, *Mystical Theology,* ch. 1; St. Thomas Aquinas, *In Boet. de Trinit.,* q. 1, a. 2, ad 1. "In finem nostrae cognitionis Deum tanquam ignotum cognoscimus".

25. [This stricture applies to the distortions in the *first* English version. Since then Charles Scribner and Sons have published a new and trustworthy translation.]

26. Cf. R. Garrigou-Lagrange, *Perfection Chretienne et Contemplation;* Jacques et Raïssa Maritain, *De la Vie d'Oraison,* new edition, Paris, Rouart, 1947, Note IV.

27. Cf. my essay "Action and Contemplation," in *Scholasticism and Politics,* New York, Macmillan, 1940.

28. Cf. R. Voillaume, *Au Coeur des masses* (*La Vie religieuse des Petits Frères du Père de Foucauld*). Paris, éd. du Cerf, 1950.